Chuck
and
the
Cowboy

Special Edition

A special printing of the second edition
featuring the artwork of Tyler Murphy

by Chuck Murphy

Cover Art & Design by Tyler Murphy

Interior Illustrations by Rosina Branger Hash

ISBN: 1-4392-1624-X
ISBN-13: 978-1-4392-1624-8

CHRIST AND THE COWBOY #2

DEAR LORD,

May the words written here and the thoughts they invoke be acceptable in your sight.

Amen

This is a second edition of *Christ And The Cowboy.* All of the poems from the original are included, plus several additional poems and short stories of a spiritual nature. It is simply a collection of some of the thoughts I as a cowboy have had over the years. May they be an inspiration to some and an enjoyment to all who read them. An appendix, with descriptions of how each piece was inspired, or came to be, has been included in the back of the book. It is always a compliment to a writer to have his work read.

Thank you.

This book is dedicated to the stewards of the land.

CHRIST AND THE COWBOY
by CHUCK MURPHY

My early childhood was on my folk's small ranch, located on the Wyoming, Montana border, at the foot of the Bighorn Mountains, east of the Little Bighorn River. The entire human environment, for the first ten years of my life, consisted of my Mom, Dad, sister, Joan, the hired man of the time, and the teacher during the winter. We were the only kids in the district so school was held there at the ranch. We were so isolated that we had to have our own tomcat. It was the worst of the Great Depression but we were so isolated that we didn't know that we were poor. During WWII, Dad sold the Little Horn Ranch and took a lease on the Crow Indian reservation in the Wolf Mountains. We later added a small deeded ranch on the Tongue River drainage to the lease and operated a family ranch corporation. Margaret and I lived our first year of married life in a cow camp on the reservation and moved to the Tongue River place the following year. That ranch was sold and the family corporation was dissolved along with Dad's retirement in '58. At that time we moved with our three children to the Bull Mountain ranch northeast of Billings, Montana where we ranched until we sold and moved to Red Lodge in 1992.

We had no spirituality in my childhood home and I don't know how I became as close to the Lord as I am. At age six I experienced my first answer to prayer. From that I knew and trusted the Father part of God. As a young adult I learned the truth of the Jesus part of God and was baptized at age 27. I became involved in our church during my thirties and changed from a growing Christian to a mechanical churchman. When that bubble burst, I became a spiritual nothing and wandered in a spiritual desert for most of my forties. At age 48, through the prayers of

4

my family, I had a personal encounter with Jesus and was grafted back to the vine. He now is not only my Lord, but also my best friend. Since that reuniting, I have learned, and am still learning about the Holy Spirit part of God.

The first and last poems in this collection were written over thirty years ago, the others more recently. It is my hope that every one who reads this booklet will receive both pleasure and spiritual insight. It is my prayer that through one of these poems Jesus will reach someone whom He could not otherwise reach.

Sincerely,

Chuck

ABOUT THE ARTISTS

COVER ARTIST & DESIGNER – TYLER MURPHY

This special printing of the second edition of Christ & the Cowboy features the cover art and design of emerging artist Tyler Murphy. Tyler is from Joliet, MT and the proud grandson of cowboy poet Chuck Murphy. He has wanted to be an artist his entire life.

Tyler's family has been instrumental in his success. They support him and encourage him to better himself. His grandfather is a source of inspiration to Tyler and has many times been the subject of his art. In fact, Chuck Murphy's image is depicted on the front and back covers of this book.

During the summer of 2008, Tyler was the Art Director for a movie filmed in Helena, MT. He has won several local and state-wide art competitions and scholarships.

In pursuit of his passion to refine and develop this talent, Tyler is enrolled at Montana State University Bozeman. Tyler is currently 18 years old.

INTERIOR ILLUSTRATOR – ROSINA HASH

Rosina Branger Hash grew up on the T O Bar Ranch in the East Rosebud Canyon at the foot of the Beartooth Mountains. It was a family livestock and dude ranch. Life on the ranch gave the Branger family the unique ability to combine people, animals, nature and God into a delightful ongoing adventure, and resulted in Rosina and Chuck's wife, Margaret, becoming life-long friends

Rosina and her husband Jack Hash ranch near Roscoe, Montana, a few miles from her home ranch. Through her art and bronze, Rosina can convey feelings in a way that few in her profession can.

Rosina's inspired illustrations accompany the poetry in this book.

ABOUT COWBOY POETRY

Cowboy poetry is usually rhyming, usually metered, usually upbeat, often tells a story or has a surprise ending. Why?

I have noticed that much non–rhyming poetry is venting anger or despair. The cowboy is the way he is by choice. If he didn't prefer being alone, he would get a higher paying job in town. He has much time to think. Even if he's with a crew or riding pens in a feedlot, his mind is on two channels. His subconscious mind tells him if an animal is sick. His conscious is thinking in words, playing with vocabulary. He instinctively wants to be happy. Rhyming, metered thoughts are more like a song in his heart and are easier to remember. The Native Americans passed their oral history from generation to generation in a chant. So the cowboy communicates with himself and others by poetry. The more alone he is the more likely he is to record his thoughts in metered rhyme.

So long as no one is hurt, the story is more important than the truth. Poetic license, stretching the blanket, is part of, "The Cowboy Way." Often cowboy poetry and stories, start with a fragment of believable truth and progress to an impossible fabrication. It is said that an old cowboy can tell you many unusual experiences, some of which are true and some of them even happened to him.

CONTENTS

RANCHER'S PRAYER OF
THANKSGIVING

Dear Lord, we give you thanks this day
For all the blessings turned our way.
We thank you for the fertile soil
That rewards us well for honest toil.
We thank you for a climate such
That this great land can grow so much.
We thank you for a government
That lets us choose the crops we plant.

Dear Lord, for help we also pray,
That you will guide us every day,
To choose our words, when speak we will.
If we should not speak, help us be still.
Help us to understand and share
The troubles that our neighbors bear.
And show us, Lord, that we may do
Each day some special task for you.

Bless please, Oh Lord, our home, our land,
Our stock, our crops, that we may stand
Proud witness in our community,
That we, Oh Lord, can work with thee.
We also ask for what it's worth,
That all your children here on earth
Could somehow have —could somehow be,
Oh Lord, as fortunate as we.

We thank you that our place of birth
Is the richest, freest place on earth.
We're thankful that we can worship you
In the special way we choose to do.
And Lord, we ask you once again,
Continue to bless those special men
Who died to keep forever free
This land for my children, wife, and me.

WHEN GOD MADE MONTANA

When God made Montana,
   He was proud what he'd done.
He made the Big Sky
   Under Montana sun.
He made the high mountains
   Their peaks capped with snow.
He made the green valleys
   And the rivers below.

When God made Montana,
   He did it with care.
He put game in the forest
   And birds in the air.
He made lakes and rivers
   And filled them with fish
And the herds of the prairie
   Completed His wish.

When God made Montana,
   He did it with pleasure.
He said, "It is good,
   I will fill it with treasure.
I will make lots of grass
   For cattle and sheep:
The minerals and oil,
   I will bury them deep."

When God made Montana,
   He said, "Yes, indeed,
This land will grow crops
   To fill human need.
I will make this great land
   In a tough, wild way,
Where the strong shall live well,
   But the weak will not stay."

When God made Montana,
   It turned out in a way
That made Him feel good,
   That He'd had a good day.
That God made Montana,
   This cowboy for one,
Will say, "Thank you, God
   For the good job you've done."

CALISTIA JANE COOLEY'S PRAYER

MY PRAYER

Dear Lord – help me –

To be patient, to dry my tears,
To show forth love, to shed all fears,
To feel the thrill of life divine,
To realize that power is mine,
To know the Christ and with Him talk,
To look for good where'er I walk,
To   do with joy each hourly task,
     This Dear Lord, is all I ask.
To banish pain, to cheer the world,
To see the flag of truth unfurled,
'Til every soul be made to see
And know his own divinity,
To realize that in each land
All war shall cease, and love shall stand,
Proclaiming peace throughout the air,
     Through all the world.
     This is my prayer.

(signed) Calistia Jane Cooley

Calistia Jane Cooley (1845–1942) was Chuck Murphy's Great
Grandmother.

GOD NEVER MADE

God never made a star
That He didn't watch at night.
God never made a sunset
That didn't fill Him with delight.

No leaf ever fell to the ground
But what God watched it fall.
All living things across this earth,
Our Father made them all.

No lightning flashed across the sky
But what God heard the thunder.
God never made a tree to grow
That He hasn't rested under.

Our Father loves all things He made
On land, sea, and sky above.
And God never made a child
That He doesn't love.

BOOTS

Here I sit in a mid–church pew
With prayer book open like I always do.
Oh me! Oh my! I just looked down.
One boot is black! One boot is brown!

I have jacket and tie and all the rest.
My shirt is clean. My pants are pressed.
I shaved this morning like I always do.
One boot is old–the other new!

Why did I not look at my feet
As I read this morning's comic sheet?
Now here I sit. Alas! Alack!
One boot is brown! One boot is black!

The thing that really makes me moan—
This morning my wife was on the phone
Putting together a special bunch
To meet some fancy place for brunch.

And I have another problem too.
At communion time, what shall I do?
With my luck it wouldn't fail;
I'd draw the center communion rail.

Folks in the aisle would surely roll
Seeing one new boot and one with hole,
Or going up, or coming back,
One boot brown and one boot black.

I swear that I wasn't over hung
From being foolish or acting young.
We had no better place to go
Than staying home with the late night show.

Sure, we shared a can of pop,
But forsook the brandy or the schnapp.
But something must have gone amiss.
Lord, am I deserving this?

You see, the boots were side by each,
Close to the bed, in easy reach,
And with my mind still in the sack,
I got one boot brown, and the other black.

In each life they say there has to be
A period of great humility.
Right now the best thing to be said,
"There's a pair like these beside my bed."

COMPUTERS IN HEAVEN

There's no computers up in heaven,
No programs, chips, or megabits,
No ROMs, or RAMs, or floppy disks.
No mouse clicks, left or right.

There's no computers up in heaven,
No modems, webs or net.
No drop–down menus,
No passwords to forget.

Anyone can access heaven,
Start up is with ease.
Anyone can access heaven
By dropping to their knees.

Any one can access heaven,
The password is the same.
To log on with Grandpa God
Just pray in Jesus' name.

If there's no computer up in heaven,
There is one thing I know,
This thing that's caused me all this hell
Has come from down below.

For my past sins I must suffer,
With hemorrhoids, corns, and gout,
Packard Bell, and Windows,
Icons, and logic turned about.

If I ever buy another computer,
Or sign up for another class,
I hope some one will take it,
And shove it up my attic.

BIRTH AND DEATH

I'll give in my cowboy logic,
My belief for what it's worth,
About the truths and mysteries
That go with death and birth.

We know before the time of birth
Life is in the mother's womb.
So I expect life in the Father's house
In the days beyond the tomb.

Birth was not the baby's choice;
He really liked it there.
With pain and trauma he left the womb
And took his first breath of air.

When forced to grow in the outside world
His body, he began to use,
To get his wants and move about.
He began to think and choose.

Now, as he grows and moves around
And explores out every room,
Think of the hell that it would be
To be confined like in the womb.

And so with the process we call death.
We shall leave our bodies behind.
We shall have pain and trauma and resist it all,
With a stubborn state of mind.

But, if release from the earthly body
Is like from the mother's womb,
It defies the imagination,
Life beyond the tomb.

RANGE BOSS

Here's a story about a cowboy
Who rode by the name of Chuck.
He'd caught self–pity pretty bad...
Felt shunned by Lady Luck.

Now, if you looked him over close,
It was pretty plain to see
That he had a close resemblance
To a feller known as me.

Well, I was riding in Carter's Coolie
When I saw this cow standing all alone,
And even from a distance
I'd guessed she'd chewed a bone.

I tightened up both cinches
And straightened out my rope
And before I got in swinging range
That cow was on a lope.

I swung and dabbed one at her
But the loop hung on her nose.
To finally get one on her,
I used up two more throws.

I jerked my slack and dallied up
And pulled her down to slow,
Then threw the slack around her hip
And spurred Buck for the throw.

The trip was nearly perfect.
My nylon stretched a yard.
She did three sixty in the air
And came down awful hard.

I grabbed three legs and wrapped 'em up,
Then called Old Buck for slack.
I stuck the fourth leg beside her neck
And told Old Buck to back.

I wedged a spur between her jaws
And pried them open wide,
And sure enough there was a bone
Way down deep inside.

Her throat was swelling on the bone;
She couldn't swallow if she tried,
And if I hadn't seen her,
That cow would sure have died.

I reached down with my fingers,
But I couldn't get a grip.
Every time I tried to pull,
My fingers just would slip.

I took off the other spur
And hooked it past the bone;
It wasn't vet procedure,
Old cow'd just lay and moan.

I finally jerked the bone out
Mid slobbers, blood and puss.
It was such an awfully smelly mess,
It tempted me to cuss.

I called Old Buck to give me slack,
Turned her loose with a touch of pride.
Next week she'd have her belly full
And her calf back by her side.

I loosened up my cinches,
And stepped back on Old Buck,
And started meditating
On this thing that we call luck.

Christ & the Cowboy, 2nd Edition

That cow herself had picked that bone,
It was her choice all the way.
When I came by and abused her so,
That was her lucky day.

I started thinking about the cowboy
That rode by the name of Chuck,
And an incident a while back;
Was it fate, or was it luck?

It seems this troubled cowboy,
The one that's known as me,
Was choked on the devil's biscuit,
Couldn't get it up or down, you see.

About then I saw a rider
Who showed up from out the blue.
He was giving me the eyeballs
Like He had a job to do.

He gave me the piercing squinters
As He rode around me twice.
I recognized him as the Range Boss
With the name of Jesus Christ.

He slapped a hooey on me,
And he jerked me to the sod,
And He gave me an injection
Of the Holy Word of God.

He removed the devil's biscuit,
And He flung it out of sight.
He was not a giant of a man,
But He was a man of might.

He put a wafer in my mouth,
And He said to chew it well.
"This is part of my body
Broke to save your soul from hell."

He put a cup up to my lips,
Said, "This looks and pours like wine,
But it really is a tonic
Made from blood of mine."

"Your name was on the cull list
To be cut out with the strays,
So if you want to graze my range,
Repent and change your ways.

"Your sins have been forgiven.
You can now get well and strong,
But I'll catch and jerk you down again
If I see you're headed wrong."

I sneaked away and shaded up
Beneath an old pine tree
And did some serious thinking
About the cowboy known as me.

And I came up mighty thankful,
As strange as it may sound,
That God's Range Boss, Jesus Christ,
Had jerked me to the ground

JOHN – FIFTEEN – ONE

Of all things said
And all scripture read
About the Father, Spirit and Son,
The one dearest to me
Just happens to be
John–Fifteen–One.

"I am the vine,"
Said Jesus Divine.
And He said that a branch am I.
And, unless I hang on tight
With all of my might,
I may be pruned, and wither and die.

So, now I can tell
That for quite a spell
I was cut off from God and His grace.
I knew what lay ahead.
I was spiritually dead
Were I not grafted back into place.

To get back I was trying
But I was broke off and dying
With no way to get back on my own.
But through unceasing prayer
Of loved ones who'd care
The mercy of Jesus was shown.

By faith without lack
They helped pray me back,
And I was grafted back to the Vine.
It felt so good to know
That the Spirit did flow
Between Christ and this body of mine.

Chuck Murphy

I remember the place.
I did not see His face.
In an embrace with His hand on my back
We stood heart to heart
Just two shirts apart
And He softly said, "Welcome back."

I looked back to see
Where my friend did once be.
There was no one, not even a sign.
There was one thing I knew,
That the prayers of love true,
Had grafted me back to the Vine.

Let it also be known
Man can't get back alone.
There is no handle on that side of the door.
There is no response from within.
It's like you never had been,
Just emptiness and nothing more.

Like the phone is dead
And no leaven in bread
And the cup just a sip of warm wine.
Who'd hear my cry?
I would wither and die
For I was severed away from the Vine.

But my family and wife
Prayed back my life.
Prayers opened the door—let me in.
Love bound the broke joint
At just the right point.
Prayers grafted me back where I'd been.

So if someone you care
Is in darkness out there,
Ask Christ if there's room for one more.
There's no handle out there,
And only through prayer,
Can Christ know to open the door.

So pray in joy and tears.
Pray for days, months and years
That a "good fruit," growing graft may be done
That your loved ones and mine
Will graft fast to the Vine
Of the Person in John, fifteen, one.

P.S. We cannot appreciate what life with Jesus is unless we experience what existence without Jesus ain't.

Chuck Murphy

LIFE WITHOUT JESUS

empty

WHEN WERE YOU SAVED

A friend of mine once asked of me
    The day that I was saved.
I was vague and non–committal
    In the answer that I gave.

There was no bolt of lightning,
    No earth nor building shook,
No great dynamic speaker,
    No song, no phrase, no book.

There was no voice from heaven,
    No light from up above.
With every little miracle
    I grew in Jesus' love.

It was an ever–growing process
    Describes my faith the best,
Like when did I acquire
    The hair upon my chest.

It's impossible to answer
    A question put like that,
Like when did I get my first gray hair
    Or when did I get fat?

But it set my mind to searching
    As questions often do,
And then the answer came to me
    So vividly, clear and true.

The year I'm a little vague on
    The day I'm certain of.
Two women were up quite early
    In a special act of love.

The man whom they were seeking
    Had departed in the night,
And sitting by His resting place
    Was an angel dressed in white.

When Jesus left the sepulcher
    And rose out from the grave...
That day, my friend and brother,
    Is the day that I was saved.

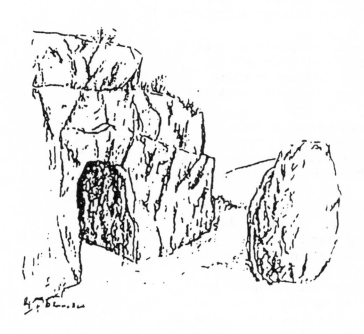

FAITH & FACTS

An eighth grade girl came home one day
    In a very upset condition.
It seemed her atheist teacher
    Had called Christ a superstition.

The teacher said, "Trust only facts
    That can be proved and measured,
And consider as myths and hearsay
    All religious beliefs once treasured."

She asked her parents for counsel
    About what she was to do,
About how to answer an atheist
    About what she knew by faith was true.

She was told to call on Jesus
    As she said her prayers that night,
And He would choose the words she'd say
    About what is true and right.

The next morning to this teacher
    She said, "I'd like to show
That what a person believes by faith
    Is stronger than what we know."

"You see that clock upon the wall?
    It tells the time of day.
It's designed and built to measure time,
    So that's a fact, you'd say."

"Yet we know it can be wrong.
    It can possibly be in error.
But, since it's probably pretty close
    We really couldn't care."

"But only by pure and simple faith
    Can a person know his mother.
She knows for certain you are her child,
    But you know by faith, none other."

"Since we cannot remember
    The moment of our birth,
Our feelings and the things we're told
    We trust for all their worth."

"But," he said, "I have a document
    With evidence to spare.
It was filled and signed by people,
    Who witnessed…who were there."

She said, "You have a document
    On which you can rely."
Then extended forth her Bible,
    And said, "And so have I."

Based on an actual experience of a teenage girl.

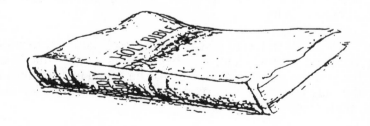

31

THE SUMMER RIDE

A fiction story that deals with some truths.

Abe sat patiently on Major as the cows and their calves strung out of the side draw and up the trail to the summer pasture. Andy, on Sergeant, followed the last old gramma cow out, and trotted up to turn back a calf that was considering showing his independence. Abe liked it when he and Andy were sent out to work together. They had been riding together for about six years now and each knew pretty much what the other was thinking. Besides Andy being good help, Abe enjoyed watching him and Sergeant work together. They had an unspoken communication that said, "If it can be done horseback, we can do it, and if it can't be done horseback, it ain't worth doing."

They came together, nodded a, "We got her done," greeting, and began to follow the cows up the trail. Andy was silent—unusual for this eleven year old. Abe waited. A question was forming. He finally broke the silence, "You got something on your mind?"

Andy looked at Abe in acknowledgment of what was said, but didn't respond for several minutes. Finally he asked, "Grandpa, have I been baptized?"

"Yeah, on the way home from the hospital, just your mom and dad, Grandma and me, and your Godparents Aunt Mary and Uncle Chris. —Why?"

"Well, Jason has to go to church every Saturday to study to be baptized, and Michael was baptized as a baby, but Jason says that you can't be baptized until you have had instruction and are old enough to make your own choice. Who's right? What is baptism all about anyway?"

"Most of us think of baptism as the sacrament of belonging. When you have been baptized in the name of the Father, Son, and Holy Spirit, you belong to Christ. —Remember the program Doc Hamilton put on about ovary transplants and how only the fertilized egg that attached to the body of the mother would survive? Well, baptism attaches you to the body of Christ." They rode in silence for a bit as each worked with his own thoughts.

"Why does Jason have to study to be baptized, and Michael and I don't?"

Abe continued. "There is another way that might be a little clearer. When you were born your folks and the doctors filled out a birth certificate that says that you are a citizen of this country. That's your birthright for being born in this country. Then they baptized you into the kingdom of God as your birthright of being born to believing parents. Remember Tye and his family? They weren't born in this country. They had to study hard, and renounce their old country to become part of this country. They probably know more about this country than you or I ever will. They had to prove that they understood this country and wanted to be part of it while your folks just claimed it as your right."

"Then what's confirmation?"

"It's the sacrament of commitment and empowerment. I like to think of it as when you apply for a job in God's vineyard. Remember when Wayne applied for the job at the feedlot? He asked me for a letter of recommendation. I said that I felt that he was old enough and sincere enough to handle the responsibility, that he had a love for that kind of work, and that he had enough knowledge and experience to do a good job. The foreman reviewed his application and references and hired him on—put him on the payroll. With confirmation, it's kind of the same. You have to have sponsors certify that you want to work for God, that you understand what the job is, and that you are the type of person that God would want on His crew. You have to do some studying before your sponsors can certify that you can handle the job. When you're ready, the bishop, one of God's foremen confirms you, hires you on."

"You said 'empowerment?' "

"Yeah, like Wayne was provided instruction, feed, medicine, and tools to look after the stock, the Holy spirit provides what you need to do God's work."

"You called baptism and confirmation sacraments. What are sacraments?"

"This is a kind of canned definition, but I don't know a better one. A sacrament is a visible sign for an invisible and spiritual grace. Like Tye, if he hadn't been granted citizenship, he would be an illegal alien. There are a lot of aliens who are enjoying some of the benefits of this country but without the papers they can't have them all. Or Wayne, he could go ride around the pens, but without being hired he wouldn't get paid."

The cows had come upon some sub-irrigated grass and stalled out for the moment. Abe felt that it would be a good time to stop, let the calves nurse, and let the animals graze. "Let's shade up a bit," he suggested as he wrapped the hobbles around his horse's front legs. "Just drop the reins on Sergeant. He won't leave with Major hobbled." They went to a shaded area and sat close to a fresh gopher mound. Abe smoothed the loose black dirt then drew a square about two inches on each side close to one edge. He drew another the same size joining it but closer to the center of his dirt tablet. To the side of this he drew another and then a fourth on the other side and a fifth opposite the first. They made a kind of plus design.

"What are you doing, Grandpa?" Andy asked.

Abe drew two more squares off the end of the last, which resulted in a total of seven squares in the shape of a cross. "Some churches consider that there are seven sacraments and they could be represented by these squares. The outside is the visible part, the inside is the invisible part, the invisible grace."

Andy looked at his grandfather, as if to say: "Go on."

"I think of the first, this top one as baptism. We talked about that. It is the only one that doesn't require a priest and that

34

uses water as the symbolic cleansing agent. Over here on the side is confirmation, the hiring on to God's crew. It requires piety, study, and an action."

"What's piety?" Andy interrupted.

"Piety is your love of God. Grace is God's love of you. As we said, you have to love God and want to work for Him, and you have to study to know how He wants things done, then the bishop confirms you, and you start to work—action. Over here on the other side is what we call the sacrament of confession or reconciliation. That is where you confess out loud things that you have done wrong. This is usually to a priest, or other spiritual director, but the important thing is that by saying it out loud to God and to another person, you hear it yourself. Then, after you have admitted your wrong, if there is a way to reconcile it you do that, and get on with life. Remember when Connie didn't feed her bum lamb and close the door to keep it warm, then when your mom asked, she said she had because she felt she would be scolded for watching TV instead of tending her chores. When your dad checked the heifers that morning the lamb was chilled, and had to be taken to the house to be saved. Connie confessed to compounding her wrongs and was truly sorry and reconciled it by changing her priorities."

"This middle one is Eucharist or Communion. It and Baptism are the only ones commanded by Jesus. We'll talk about it later. This one in the middle of this upright post is Marriage. The top five are all general sacraments, involving most people. The bottom two are, well, more special purpose sacraments." He paused briefly. "Marriage is the most important decision that a person ever makes in a life time. Marriage is to decide and commit to love one person for the rest of your life. Marriage is to decide to share one's possessions, time, body, goals, dreams; one's entire life with a chosen mate."

"What about divorce?"

"I've had a lot of trouble with divorce. 'Till death do us part.' For a long time I thought that only a medical doctor could declare one of the two people dead. I had thought for a long time that a marriage only involved two people. But a true marriage involves a man, a woman, and God. When the man and woman fail to include God in their marriage, it is like they never were married. They are just legally living together. When the God part of the marriage dies, the judge declares the marriage dead, and it is like the man or woman died except there are two to grieve."

"But really good people get divorced."

"God's spirit doesn't have to leave the people, it just dies in that marriage." He thought a moment. "Remember last summer when we watched the Indians putting up the teepee? They tied two poles together, then tied a third to them and then stood the three up. Each pole supported the other two. If they were not properly bound, all three would fall. If one pole is not solid and breaks, it all falls down. Each pole is independent and must stand on its own, except for the point of being tied to the other two. It must support the other two, yet be supported by them. It's the same with marriage. Man must support his wife and God, and woman must support man and God. If they each support God, God will support them. Then remember how other poles were placed against the first three. These could be like jobs, children, homes, debt, parents, church, community, and friends. If they are balanced around the first three, the teepee takes shape and the covering is well supported. If these other poles were not balanced, it would get lopsided and collapse, but with each in its proper place the canvas is well supported and a warm shelter is built."

"What was this middle one again?"

"Communion. Some call it Eucharist or Mass. You know how we believe that God can do any thing? Well, we believe that God will transform the bread and wine into the body and blood of Christ. You know, like we say, black soil and clear water make green grass, which makes red meat. Well, God changes the wafer and wine into the body and blood of Christ much the same way."

"But how does that help us?"

"Remember last winter when we vaccinated the cows so that the calves wouldn't get sick when they were born? It didn't make the cow sick, but she built up a resistance that passed on to the calf. Well, Christ came to earth to be exposed to human sin. He didn't sin himself but he allowed his body to be mutilated by man. Then he promised to transform bread and wine into that sin–conditioned body. That works like the calf getting antibodies from the cow, we will get protection from the sins of the world. Communion is like a vaccination against the ungodly."

"I see... I think. What are these other two?"

"This one is called Ordination. It's like a power of attorney for God."

"Power of attorney?"

"Yeah, a power of attorney gives some one the power, the right, to do certain things for another. When my mother got old, she gave me power of attorney in all her affairs. That didn't mean that she loved me more, or that I loved her more than my sisters or brother, only that I knew a little more about her business, and that I was chosen to look after her affairs. Certain people study God's business, are willing to take the responsibility, and are chosen, ordained, to do his work. They don't love God more than you or I. They may be in closer contact, but God loves us all the same."

"This last one I think has changed since I was a kid. When I was first learning about the sacraments it was called Extreme Unction or Last Rites, and was for the dying. Now it's called Healing, and is for those who ask God's help to keep living— keep well."

"I better get around that old red–necked cow before we both get fired," Andy said as he reached for Sergeant's reins.

"Yeah, enough of God's vineyard, we had better get back to our jobs."

[Grandpa's Drawing]

Baptism
Confirmation Communion Confession
Marriage
Ordination
Unction

Chuck Murphy

COWBOY'S VIEW ON ABORTION

When a cow aborts we never laugh;
We simply say, "She slinked her calf."
But a trend with people has me appalled.
Planned abortion is what it's called.

It makes me think of a man I know
And a case two thousand years ago.
A girl named Mary could have died in shame
Even though she had not played the game.

Said Joseph, "I must choose
Between having her stoned by righteous Jews
Or simply leave well enough alone
And raise her bastard child as my own."

An angel told Mary to bare the shame
And even told her the baby's name.
Then he went and talked with Joe.
Said, "Raise the child and let him grow."

Who tells girls to have abortions now?
The one who gave Eve the forbidden chow?
Who can of his own free will
Say an unborn child I'm going to kill?

Where would our world be today,
Had Mary gone the abortion way,
Had she chosen to abort,
Had Jesus' mission been cut short?

Today it may not be a virgin birth,
But a fetus has life, and life has worth.
I shudder to think of life on earth
Had Jesus not had a normal birth.

ONCE UPON A TIME

Once upon a time about two thousand years ago;
Once upon a time is how stories start you know;
There were three fellers who thought themselves as kings.
Who were camel jockeys, with myrrh, and gold, and things.

They had come a long way. They had traveled far,
Guided by light from heaven, which they thought was a star.
There was a sheep herder, on night guard with his sheep,
But the light was different, and kept him from his sleep.

He went down to the barn, to kind of check things out,
To see what was going on, what the light was all about.
In a manger among the critters, a little baby lay,
Sleeping peacefully, on a bed of fluffed up hay.

The camel jockeys came with gifts of myrrh and gold,
A little out of character for Easterners of old.
They had an attack of generosity on this winter night,
And gave gifts to the baby to start his life of right.

'Cause this light from heaven, away up in the sky,
Came direct from Father God, the sparkle in His eye.
Father God was happy, overfilled with joy.
He'd just had His only child, a little baby boy.

You'd expect God's Son be born in some exalted place,
But a bunch of barnyard critters were first to see his face.
God tired of kings and emperors, the evil they had done.
So He sent a messenger. He sent His Only Son.

That babe received some earthly gifts, of frankincense, of gold,
The gifts that He gave back to earth, increased ten million fold.
Jesus gave us love, and hope; Oh, where does one begin,
And health, and peace, and faith, and forgiveness of our sin.

He told of Our Father's house, the place where He would be,
How He'd prepare a camp for us, a place for you and me,
A place filled with good things, beauty, song, and laughter,
Where all who believe in Him will live happily ever after.

FAITHFUL ONE

We can learn so many lessons
    From animals with which we live.
They demand and ask so little
    Yet have so much to give.

A cowboy is in the middle
    Between his dog and his Lord,
And in between the two of them
    A world of truth is stored.

If I could serve God the Father
    The way my dog serves me
I'd be assured a place in heaven
    For all eternity.

My dog couldn't really help me
    If he were on a leash.
I also believe man's freedom
    Is God the Father's wish.

My dog will go out after steers
    As far as he can see.
He couldn't serve me half as well
    If he were chained to me.

I see men whose wives and children
  Are emotionally chained and bound
By a man who dominates their lives
  Determined to hold them down.

Yes, my dog can serve me best
  When he's free to bark and run.
And the only pay he ever asks
  Is to know the job's well done.

So, Dear Lord, please help me
  To let those I love be free
To go in pursuit of greater things,
  As far as they can see.

And when my earthly steer–chasing days
  Are finished up and done,
May I lie and rest beside His chair
  And be called, "Faithful One."

HOW I PRAY

I looked at the clock as I opened my eyes;
Four forty–five in the morning was not a surprise.
It's part of a habit for starting the day.
"Come Holy Spirit, come help me pray."

"Forgive me, Lord Jesus, for all of my sins,"
Is how my morning prayer usually begins.
"Forgive me my sins, both known and unknown.
Forgive the indifference I know I have shown.

I thank you, Lord Jesus, for being the one
Who greeted me back as the prodigal son.
For forgiving me, Jesus, as only you can
When as Peter, I said, "I don't know the man."

I praise you, Lord Jesus, for the good things in life;
My children, grandchildren, my friends, and my wife.
I thank you and praise you for blessing them all,
In all their endeavors, both large and small.

But how can I praise you for things I like not
Like the failure to reach a goal that I sought?
Can I thank you for a corn that truly does hurt
Until I see a man without legs drag himself in the dirt?

Or give thanks that my home costs so much to heat
Until I think of the people who live in the street?
Or that the cost of driving continues to grow
Unless I pray for the millions with nowhere to go ?

Can I thank you for the struggle to control my weight
And forget those who can't remember the last meal
      they ate?
How can I praise you with all of my heart
When a dream castle crumbles and falls all apart?

I can get up and praise you each time I fall
When I think of the millions with no dream at all.
Thank you, Lord Jesus, for this special way
That you enter my life at the start of my day.

Thank you, Lord Jesus, for this time of ours.
Today I'll hear a bird sing and smell a few flowers.
With your help, I'll walk the extra mile,
Help the stranger across the aisle,

Comfort a child who bruised a knee,
Help someone more clearly see.
So please through me let your light shine
To honor the Father—yours and mine.

BLIND

A lot of snow has fallen since I found the blind calf on the rock ledge nearly thirty years ago. In that time I have had many thoughts related to the lessons learned in that experience. That day my mind had been mostly concerned with the lay service that I was to conduct at church the next day. I was a poor reader and worse at singing. It seemed that the whole thing was an act of penance and endurance for both me, and the congregation. The singing was the worst, those old hymnal pieces were hardly sounds from heaven.

I had made most of my circle starting the calves to the feedlot. It had snowed about three inches the afternoon before, with enough wind to shake it out of the trees and clear the rocks and bare ground. I had ridden out on a rocky point when I saw a lone calf on a rock ledge some three hundred yards away. I rode as close as I could, dismounted, and climbed down to where he was. He had gotten over a rounded sandstone ledge about three feet high. There was a crack in the rock that he could have gotten up if he could have found it. Downward escape would have been to fall about five feet over another rounded edge to the grass and rocks below. The space that he was trapped on was about ten feet by fifteen feet, or about the size of an average bedroom. I could see where he had licked some snow for moisture, and had eaten the few bites of coarse grass at the base of the upper ledge. He was gaunt, dehydrated, and had probably been there for two or three days. His biggest problem was that he was totally blind in both eyes.

I knew that my horse couldn't pull him back up over the ledge, and felt the best rescue effort was for him to jump down and make his way to open ground out the bottom. As I tried to encourage him to jump, I realized that he had no idea of how far it would be, and that he would feel like he was falling off the edge of the world. I maneuvered him to the area above the least rocks and pushed him off. My heart filled with compassion as I tried to imagine the fear of falling into the unknown.

In disoriented panic he scrambled to his feet and tried to escape this monster that had pushed him into this new field of obstacles and hazards. He bumped into trees and large rocks, and stumbled over the smaller rocks and down logs.

It took several minutes to get back to my horse and ride around the rim to where he was. He had stumbled into a more open park, and I began to talk to him. He moved away from my voice and eventually learned that he could walk slowly without falling by taking high steps. I could have roped him at this time, but his fighting the rope would have been harder on him than falling over invisible hazards. I stayed fifty to seventy–five feet away, moving wide to either side, and by keeping a constant voice reference, I was able to maneuver him out onto an open meadow with no obstacles. From there, we had to negotiate a hundred foot wide pass in the rim.

I had switched to some cowboy songs to maintain a consistent sound, and he would move with some confidence. He soon learned that when my voice changed to words, an obstacle was eminent and he would be more cautious. At the top of the little pass we hit a trail used by the other calves. He became more sure of himself, feeling the trail with his feet and turning back when he felt the undisturbed snow on the side. Soon the calves that had already gathered at the feed lot began to bawl in response to my voice. The blind calf perked up in recognition of the sound of his kind. He knew that he had a chance if he could once more get with the herd. The other calves had drunk enough to cause the pump to start, and when the blind calf heard the cadence of the pump jack he turned to the tank and drank deeply.

By the time I had the grain in the troughs he was mixed into the herd never to be isolated again. He didn't regain his sight but traveled with the others and was marketed with the rest of the herd.

This is the end of the story as far as the calf, but it has affected my life for over thirty years. I shared the story with the few dedicated in the pews the next day, and have prayed many times that the combined voices of the faithful would call some blinded person home.

I remember the anguish in my heart as I pushed the frightened calf over the edge of the rock, and think of the anguish of Father God, as he pushes some of His children into frightening circumstances to save their souls.

I have related the expression, "An isolated Christian is an ineffective Christian," to the fact that the calf would have died by himself. But, when reunited with others of his kind, he did as well as they in spite of his handicap.

I saw the relationship to what happened then, and what we call, "Tough Love," in family situations of today.

I have meditated on the parallel in the fact that the calf first went to water, and that baptism is our first step toward life in our Father's house.

And so a blind calf helped me see God's wonders.

© Rosina

MONEY

A man said something I thought odd,
That a certain person had more money than God.
He said it as a kind of joke,
But, cash wise God is broke.
Since the very start of time,
God hasn't had a crying dime.

God told Moses, cast in stone,
That as God, He was alone.
So the truth is plain and real,
God had no peers with whom to deal.
With nothing to buy, it's almost funny,
To think of God as having money.

With God no treasure chests are found,
He mixed His diamonds in the ground.
He had no use for rings of gold,
Or gem studded crowns to behold.
With a little thought, there is no doubt,
Grandpa God is cash without.

With no material assets about which to boast,
Just what then, does God treasure most?
He treasures most, for all it's worth,
The love of his children here on earth.
He said that a jealous God He'd be,
Jealous of the love of you and me.

To love him with all our soul and heart
Is where God's commandments start
He gives His love to me and you,
A gift of kind is the least we can do.
Yes, it may seem rather odd,
We all have more money than Grandpa God.

FIRST THESSALONIANS: 5–26 KJV

Through out the Holy Word of God
Are commandments, rules, and law,
And if we'd know and obey them all,
Our lives would not have flaw.

Jesus taught us how to pray
In Matthew six, verse nine.
In Mark (10:15), "Become as children
If you are to be one of mine."

Then ways of Christian action
By which our lives to build,
Paul in his epistles,
Books of rules are filled.

Now, Paul was a male chauvinist,
Not kind to our fairer sex.
Most of what he said to them
Was to keep their place in check.

There is one of his commandments
I've not heard from the altar.
That it's among my favorites
Is a fact I will not falter.

It's aimed at the fair and lovely
To keep Christ's Church alive:
First Thessalonians: verse twenty six
At the end of chapter five. (KJV)

"Greet all the brethren with an holy kiss."

PLATELETS

You walk in the Blood Services door,
Head for the men's room below,
'Cause you know it's going to be a while
'Til you have another chance to go.

You give your card to the front desk girl,
She asks if you've changed your name,
If you are who you say you are,
And if your address is the same.

Then they take you to a little booth
And invite you to have a chair.
They ask if you are feeling good,
And the last time you were there.

They ask if you've had syphilis,
Or been involved in sex for pay,
Or taken any steroids,
Or partied with a man that's gay.

When you've answered all the questions,
And at last the page is full,
You come to the conclusion,
That your life is down–right dull.

They have you read a line aloud
To prove that you are smart,
Then take your pulse and pressure
To prove you have a heart.

They stick a thing into your mouth,
Your temperature to read,
Then stab you in the finger
To see if you will bleed.

When they're fully satisfied
About the mundane life you live,
That you're alive and breathing,
And your blood is fit to give,

Then they take you to the donor room,
And you lay back in a chair.
They again ask what your name is,
And when you first breathed air.

They take blood from your right arm
And it goes through a machine
That makes a kind of whirring noise
And has a computer screen.

The machine separates the platelets,
Seven hundred trillion, more or less,
Then through a tube in your left arm
It gives you back the rest.

It takes about ninety minutes,
Give or take a few.
You visit with the technicians
And tell a lie or two.

Some times they get busy
And you have time to meditate,
About how God has blessed you
In the direction of your fate.

He's given you an abundance,
More platelets than you need,
To not share this abundance
Would be an act of greed.

Christ & the Cowboy, 2nd Edition

The receiver of this abundance
Sure owes no thanks to you,
To give back of God's goodness
Is the least that you can do.

It seems that this abundance
Is a little like God's grace,
Whenever some is taken,
There is more to take its place.

To share of this abundance
From the marrow of my bone,
Is a way of saying, "Thank you God,"
For the goodness you have shown,

ROSES ARE RED

Roses are red.
Violets are blue.
Christ died on the cross
For me and for you.

Roses are red.
Lilies are white.
He died for us
To set our sins right.

Blue is the violet.
Red is the rose.
On Easter morning
From the tomb He arose.

Violets are blue.
Roses are red.
That Christ is our savior,
Is all there is to be said.

© Rosina

LANDMARK

Proverbs 22:28

"Remove not the forefathers' landmark,"
Those were the words that I read.
"Remove not the forefathers' landmark,"
That's what the "Good Book" said.

The old cabin to me was a landmark.
It had become an ugly has–been,
A shack, a revolting eyesore.
Where it once housed families and workers
Now it sheltered dogs, nothing more.

"Remove not the forefathers' landmark."
The words dug deep in my heart
As the tractors flexed their muscles
To tear the old landmark apart.

The forefathers could have watched proudly.
The old cabin was sturdy and sound,
For a fairly good log chain was broken
Before the first log hit the ground.

I'll save a piece of the landmark,
That is the least I can do.
I'll save a piece of the landmark,
Some brick and a good log or two.

For this ugly old landmark
Had no use, was just in the way.
Though my heart strings cried for its history,
I really had nothing to say.

So, now it's burned and destroyed,
Cremated, gone for good.
Now garden plants are sprouting
Where once the old landmark stood.

We removed the forefathers' landmark
Be it right or wrong, it is true.
We removed the forefathers' landmark,
But we sure did improve the view.

SOMEBODY'S GRANDMOTHER'S CHAIR

Inspired by Linda Cheney

I felt the chill in the November air
As we went to pick up a broken old chair.
Her husband had teased her with comments to spare,
But she wanted, and bought, that broken old chair.

In an old homestead shack abandoned for years,
A Montana tribute to sweat, courage, and tears.
She first saw it on a brisk morning stroll,
And craved it, though time had taken its toll.

There was junk and trash all over the floor
And an old broken chair beside the door.
I looked for something of value there,
Then she asked me to load that broken old chair.

The finish long gone, a spring was lacked,
The veneer was peeling, the frame was cracked,
But she was as thrilled as she could be,
For she'd seen something that I couldn't see.

She said, "How could anyone leave it there?
It was somebody's Grandmother's rocking chair.
Sure it needs refinished, and some repair,
But it's somebody's Grandmother's rocking chair."

In a time when hospitals and doctors were rare,
Health was maintained in that old rocking chair,
And God has listened to many a prayer
Silently spoken from that old chair.

Like the waves clean the beach
But go nowhere,
Souls were cleansed, cares removed ,
Rocked away in that chair.

The hurts of the day
And the thoughts of despair,
Became hope and joy
Rocked to life in that chair.

I helped box it up with a reverent air,
This once only junk,
But now treasured chair,
And I felt great respect for the woman who'd dare
To restore, "Somebody's Grandmother's Rocking Chair."

MEANING OF CHRISTMAS

I got to meditating
"What Christmas really means..."
Is it brightly wrapped packages,
Bright lights, and Christmas greens?

What does Christmas really mean
To folks like me and you?
Is it too much hustle and bustle
 With too many things to do?

Is it planning to have some special time
To spend with loved ones dear?
Is it sending off a boughten card
To one forgotten for a year?

What about the white haired lady
In a nursing home wheel chair,
Dependent on a hired aid
For all her needs and care

And I think about a homeless man,
In a box, down on skid row.
He'll have dinner at The Mission
With no better place to go.

Our heads shake in frustration
Wondering what to do for him.
We say his past was wasted
And his future at best is dim.

What does Christmas really mean
To a person in his place?
While others with high spirits
Celebrate our Savior's grace?

He sees decorations atop a penthouse
Silhouetted against the sky,
A place where rich and famous
Live comfortably and high.

He thinks about his mother,
When he sat upon her knee
As she read about a baby
Sent to set believers free.

How when that child had grown up
He told us what He'd do;
He'd prepare a place in heaven,
A place for me and you.

Way down deep inside his heart
This vagrant person knows,
When he's judged before his Maker
It won't be by his clothes.

Once again he tells himself
What he's known all along,
You need only to love Lord Jesus
To get where you belong.

There are no credit cards in heaven
No limousine, jets, or halls of fame.
In heaven everybody walks
And all men speak the same.

So Christmas has a meaning
More than gifts beneath a tree.
Christmas means a babe was born
To set believers free.

GRANDPA GOD

An acquaintance said she thought it odd
That I call The Creator, "Grandpa God."
Right then about all that I could say,
Was, "I guess it's just the, 'The Cowboy way.' "

When I first heard it, I don't know.
It was probably forty or fifty years ago.
It says how we feel about God today,
How we feel, The Cowboy Way.

See, in the beginning, Creator God,
Was hard and demanding, rode roughshod.
People trembled and called Him, "Lord."
And pictured Him with a mighty sword.

But then The Creator had a Son,
Who came and lived with us as one.
Jesus saw God a different way,
And called Him, "Father," when He'd pray.

So God became, "Our Father," then,
And was seen as a loving God by men.
He was kinder, more forgiving,
Abba God, to all the living.

Now the Son of God has died,
And is seated by Our Father's side.
He helps The Creator watch o'er the fold
As God takes more of a Grandpa role.

So as I reach my grandpa days,
I see life in different ways.
With all my grand kids, my love is true,
Though I may not like some things they do.

I must let each child independent be
To be themselves and grow up free.
And if they come to talk or share
I'll want to listen, I'll be there.

And so it is with Grandpa God.
He knows the trails we have trod.
He knows when we fell and got back up
He has fed us through the Bread and Cup.

He may not like how we behave
But He will forgive us to the grave,
If only we confess that we did wrong
And we knew He loved us all along.

So may, "He," my role model be.
May Jesus Christ my mentor be.
May I hear what He has to say
And worship Him, The Cowboy Way.

And if from Grandpa God we stray,
He hopes to welcome us back some day.
But if the bridge of Grace is burned,
We lose the inheritance we haven't earned.

So when I call Him, "Grandpa God."
I don't think it the least bit odd.
To call Him Grandpa when I pray,
Well, that's just the "Cowboy Way."

CONE TREE

"We need Christmas greenery," the voice said on the phone.
"We really need pine boughs, especially those with cone."
I found a big old wolf tree on the field edge all alone.
It seemed that every branch was clustered full with cone.

The edge of my field is not my favorite place for trees,
If I cut it down, I could snap the boughs with ease.
I fired up the chain saw and said unto the tree,
"I'm sorry about this, my friend. It will hurt you more than me."

Then I thought I heard it answer, "Yes, I'm sure that it will smart,
But to give my life for Jesus, I can do with all my heart."
I really did a double–take and looked around to see
If any one had caught me talking to a tree.

It said, "Here on this field's edge, I'm only in the way.
I take up the moisture that you need for grain and hay.
I'm not tall and straight enough to be cut into a board,
And I would die most proudly to glorify the Lord."

"Jesus stretched wide his arms when He died for man
I spread my branches for Him with all the pride I can.
You understand, to a tree life's greatest worth
Is to help celebrate The Savior's birth."

Like the Roman sword in Jesus side,
The chain saw roared, and the Cone Tree died.
So that the tree not have died in vain,
God bless this home in Jesus name.

@ Rosina

YOUNG WOMAN

The young woman at the podium
Seemed so pretty, young, and pure.
She was trying to verbalize for us
God's faithfulness to her.

She told how in her college years,
She from God's will had strayed,
Then when her life hung by a thread,
The bargain she had prayed.

She told of how her mother
Was stricken—cancer's way.
And of how the fam–i–ly
Had gathered 'round to pray.

Then how a special beam of light
Had caused a rainbow there.
And she knew by the rainbow
That God had heard their prayer.

Why her mother did recover,
The doctors didn't know.
Yet, it's plain to us believers
In the promise of the bow.

She told how for thirty minutes
Before the break of day,
She clears her life of other things
To meditate and pray.

She told how a lighted candle
Would set her mood to pray.
How she placed one in the window
Before the break of day.

That glass can cause reflections
Is really nothing new.
But as she did her morning prayer,
The candle light was two

God had brought his candle
Before the break of day,
To share the thirty minutes
She had set aside to pray.

It was a message that I needed,
God's faithfulness to her,
For even in His vineyard,
I felt forgotten and unsure.

I was feeling isolated,
Removed from Christian friend,
In the out–back of His vineyard
With a lonely life to spend.

So, Lord in the morning
When ice from the trough is thrown,
May I look in the water and see a face
And know I'm not alone.

For I am sure that as with her,
You , Lord, will faithful be.
If I set aside some time for prayer,
You will be here with me.

MY WALK IN FAITH

"I just can't buy into this Jesus/God stuff. I wish I could. I'm sorry." The person was sincere. He didn't want to be a hypocrite. It just didn't fit together.

It made me think back over my own spirituality. My Dad was agnostic. He just couldn't accept the virgin birth. If he couldn't accept that, what was there to build on? Mom read the Bible some, but we never discussed any thing spiritual in our home. I don't remember any one ever praying with me. We never went to church. We put up a tree and had gifts and candy at Christmas. We had ham and sweet potatoes on Easter. The ever–changing troupe of ranch help often referred to God. Some in profanity, some with respect. Sis and I were the only kids in the school district so I wasn't exposed to peers with religious training. I can remember some one refuting the Bible by saying, "Oh sure, and they all thought the world was flat then, too." How, then, did my faith evolve?

I think back to when I was six years old. Mom was to have supper for the thrashing crew that would be coming that afternoon. She asked me to catch and kill the chickens that she planned to cook. I caught two nice young roosters and put them under a washtub. I needed to drive two nails into the chopping block to hold their heads. I got the nails and Dad's favorite hammer from the shop and performed the executions with the double–bitted ax and took the result to Mom. When I went back to return Dad's hammer, it was nowhere to be found. I had committed an unforgivable sin. I searched along the big log that I was sure I had placed it on. I felt in the chips around the chopping block. I searched in the grass beside the big log. I went back to the shop to see if I taken it back, hoping this was just a bad dream.

In desperation, I fell on the hired man's bed and prayed, "God if you will help me find Dad's hammer, I will thank you a thousand times." (I remember that prayer to this day.) I went back to look again and there it was on the big log where I was sure it was. It was there in plain view. I started back to the shop with the hammer, saying, "Thank you, God. Thank you, God. Thank you, God. Thank you, God. ..." Under normal circumstances, it would have been knocked off while I was searching there, but with God or God's angels, anything can happen. I repeated, "Thank you, God," over and over as I went out to bring in the milk cows and was gathering the eggs. God must have smiled as He looked down at a little six year old boy trying to keep his share of a bargain with Him.

I didn't understand it, but prayer worked. I guess it was like a match that when pulled across the plate of the stove, would burst into flame. The match would light the paper, the paper would light the kindling, the kindling would light the wood, the wood would light the coal, and Mom would cook breakfast. Some times the match wouldn't light. Some times prayers weren't answered, but matches and prayers worked most of the time, and I began to use both or either as needed. Subconsciously, I believed that if prayers were answered, there was a person or power that did the answering. So I called that power, God.

For the sixth grade I boarded with a family at Wyola, Montana. I had to stay down over the weekend once, so I went to church with them. It was my first time in a church. It was kind of scary and we whispered like we didn't want God to know we were there. Later, when we moved into Sheridan Wyoming, for us kids to be in a bigger school system, I found that the kids that I liked, and wanted to associate with, went to Sunday School. I accepted the invitation to attend, and a little bit of formal religion must have rubbed off. I had no commitment and went where the cutest girls were. I chose to associate with peers that had spiritual roots. I learned about Moses and the commandments in stone. One of the Sunday School teachers had a thing about David. I thought he was a whimpering coward who had no conscience. He did write some good stuff like the 23rd Psalm. I had to memorize John 3:16.

Still, my faith was in God, and the rest I accepted because others believed. I still had prayers answered like the time my horse fell on me and we slid 45 feet as he came over me. I prayed, "God save me." I should have been killed but not a bone was broken. As I reached upper teen years, I began to see how Jesus had to come and show us how to live...and how to die, not just so we could celebrate Christmas and Easter. Another prayer to God was answered so vividly that only God could have done it. In my mid–twenties, I felt the urge to study and learn more, and to work in the church. At age 27, I was baptized to the body of Christ. I was getting a full–blown case of religion. By my mid–thirties, I was worshipping the church and forgetting God. Prayers were no longer answered. I consulted with people of God, but my communication with God was cut off. Then one day at the table of some friends, I said, "I think that I'll go back to being a heathen. God answered my prayers then, but now with all this Bible and Jesus stuff nothing is working." I remember thinking that this was the third time I had said this, and a little rooster crowed in my subconscious. Well, God didn't like that very much and gave me the silent treatment for several years. Finally my wife and family prayed me back. Jesus is real and alive and is my best friend. The Spirit, referred to as The Helper in the Bible, is just that and will do any thing Jesus asks Him to do. Prayers are answered, not all, but like the matches, most of them.

I believe that God sent an angel to blind a little six–year–old boy so that child would believe in Him. So to sum up my faith, if prayers are answered, who does it? God. If God can answer prayers, He can do any thing else that He wants to do. I denied Him once, and that was a BIG mistake. So I have come full circle and again believe as a child. (Matthew 18:1-6)

P. S. It takes action to strike a match. Likewise, sometimes it takes action on our part for God to have the means to answer our prayers.

CAUGHT

I lay in bed this morning
Before the rising of the sun,
Thinking about how things will be
When my walk on earth is done.

Here our misdeeds are judged
Only if we're caught.
But there we will be judged
On the evil things we thought.

Will an angel pull my folder
Down from off the shelf
And say, "The way you treat your neighbor
You must really hate yourself."

Have I really loved my Grandpa God
With all my heart and mind,
When to all the needs around me
I'm insensitive and blind.

Up in heaven we'll be judged
For every sin of thought,
And can't feel we are innocent
Because we were not caught.

WHO AND WHAT

A friend of mine once told his son
As the boy stood at the door,
"Remember who you are, Son,
And the things you're standing for."

Then he told how some time later
Things were turned about.
That night, the boy was staying home,
And the Dad was going out.

And the boy said, "Dad, remember
The words you said to me,
About the things you stand for,
And the man you're cut to be."

It made me stop and question,
"How have I played my hand?
Have I really lived and practiced
The things for which I stand?"

And today again I wonder,
"Just what will be the score
When my work on Earth is over,
And I reach that distant shore?"

Have I had the perseverance
To be the man I should?
Have I used wisdom and good judgment
In the things for which I stood?

What will be my answer
When I knock on 'That Great Door'
And St. Peter calls out, "Who are you
And what have you stood for?"

WOMEN OF THE CHURCH

There were Christian Crusades
And Viking raids.
Oh, those men were a hearty crew.
They were rugged men
With a passionate yen
To do what they had to do.

They would do battle and die
Yet not question why
The battle was being fought.
They would storm up a hill
To die or to kill
Just because they felt they ought.

But all tales told
About the brave men of old
Are out classed in every way
By the sweet smelling things
With their bracelets and rings,
The women of the Church today.

'Cause a man could be killed
For interrupting a Guild
Making things for the coming bazaar.
So this cowboy has found
To not tred their ground
And belong to his church from afar.

'Cause those sweet smelling things,
With their bracelets and rings
That are so warm and cuddly to hug,
Can get a curl in their lip,
And shoot straight from the hip
When it comes to choosing a rug.

They have voices so sweet
Until they start choosing the meat
That will be served at the next bazaar lunch.
Then voices get rude
And fangs protrude
Until agreement is reached by the bunch.

But in a moment of jest
Let a husband suggest
They serve sandwiches made of sardines.
He'd be butchered and diced
And sautéed and spiced
Then fed to the hogs without greens.

So a mystery they'll stay
Until the end of the day—
The women who make the church run.
So I'll love 'em and hug 'em
And help 'em and bug 'em
'Cause the women of the church are more fun.

AUCTION BARN

This particular day
It was right on my way
To stop at the Auction Barn,
Just to check for now
On the price of a cow
And to see what I could learn.

So I took a seat
And rested my feet
On the back of the one in front,
And I fixed my gaze
On the passing maze
Of what the buyers didn't want.

The feeder steers were full,
And their eyes were dull.
The PA was turned up loud.
My eyes did stray
Across the way
Seeing who was in the crowd.

There was George and John,
And the list went on,
To Bill, and his good wife Sue.
There was Slim and Jack
But my eyes came back
To a stranger as they often do.

He was eyeballing me
Like I had to be
A critter from outer space,
With a steely stare
That would raise your hair
And made me turn my face.

He had a disarming air
That would stampede a bear,
This salty old line–camp goat.
He had a chew in his jaw
Like a turkey's craw
And a black silk scarf round his throat.

His face was brown,
And he wore a frown,
And white as a cloud was his hair.
His nose was long,
And his jaw was strong.
His shoulders were broad and square.

He wore a Levi jean
That a saddle had seen,
And could almost stand alone,
And a jacket to match
With a canvas patch
That was harness needle sewn.

His hat was worn,
And the brim was torn
And stained by wind and weather,
With a double wide band
Of sixteen strand
Braided English lacing leather.

The scar on his chin
Told me that he'd been
More than one time in a brawl.
I bet a week's pay
In his younger day
He'd have been a tough man to call.

Then up he stood
Straight as finish wood,
And he started to walk my way.
He was a man of brawn
And his gut was drawn
Like he's lived many a hungry day.

His legs were bowed
From the horses he'd rode
When his bones were young and soft.
He'd breathed his share
Of nicotine air
I could tell by the way he coughed.

The hurt in his hip
Caused a twinge in his lip.
The ache in his joints was real.
It was very plain
That the man had pain
From his head to his run over heel.

But he stood up proud
As he came through the crowd
And seated himself at my right.
He stared like a judge,
And I didn't budge
As he eyed my size and height.

He said "I think, lad,
That I worked for your dad
On that place up the Little Horn.
We had tough ways
In the depression days
Shortly after you were born.

"It's hard to keep track
When it's that far back;
The exact year I don't recall."
Then said without laugh,
"It was a year and a half
That I worked for Old Pat that fall."

"Old Pat was one
To not hurry you none
In the work he lined out for the day.
In wind, sun or shower
You could have eighteen hour
In which to earn your pay."

Over an hour this goat
With the scarf round his throat
Rattled on in picturesque prose.
He'd flip his chew in his cheek
Each time that he'd speak,
And he'd end with a sniff of the nose.

His voice was quite gruff
Like he'd had quite enough
Of the liquid you buy in a bar.
My guess was
He'd had many a buzz
From the clear stuff you'd get in a jar.

He said he'd told Dad
Of the lean times he'd had—
That there was no work where he'd been.
He had a hole in a shoe.
His clothes were not new.
His blankets were tattered and thin.

Said, "Pat didn't care
About the blankets he'd wear.
The rest could be left in the trunk."
Pat said, "You'll soon see
If you're working for me
You'll spend damn little time in the bunk."

Then he said he'd had word
That Pat had a herd
Across that Great Divide.
Said he wished for Old Pat
That his steers were all fat
And he had long gaited horses to ride.

Now by the timing of fate
They opened the gate
And let some dandy brood cows in the ring.
There was a hush in the crowd
And the PA was loud

79

As the auctioneer started to sing.

I just got the jitters
As I looked at them critters.
How I wished that my bankroll was fat.
And my blood ran cold
When the man said, "Sold —
To that man in the Panama hat."

I turned back to review
The man with the chew.
He was gone like a thief in the night.
I quick filled with shame
For I had not asked the name
Of the stranger who'd sat on my right.

I checked the coffee shop
To see if he'd stop
For a cup of Annabelle's brew.
I checked the lobby and can,
But could not find the man
With the scarf and the oversized chew.

So, Dear Lord, lay your hand
On that salty old man.
Take his hurts, Dear Lord, take them all.
Dear Lord, I pray
That you bless this day,
The man who worked for my Dad that fall.

WALK

Doc sat me on the table
And says, "We got to talk.
If I'm to keep you healthy,
You'll have to learn to walk."

I sat silent for a bit, then looked him in the eye.
And in all sincerity, I says, "Why?"
He flipped through my file like a doctor often does
And said with authority in his voice, "Cause!"

I says, "But Doc, walking
Ain't a cowboys favorite thing to do.
The critters God made for walking
Has four legs 'stead of two.

"Birds is made for flying.
There's no way to drown a fish.
Horses for moving cowboys,
Was the Creator's wish."

He says, "Your tests here
Show your health ain't at a peak,
You got enough lard in your blood
To grease your tractor for a week.

"You huff and, puff and, wheeze and, grunt
And say your joints all ache,
 So it is time you loose some weight
And gave your heart and joints a break.

"Your muscles are like wet noodles,
Your belly hides your belt,
You sure are in no shape at all
To play the hand you're dealt.

"You have to many triglycerides
In your arteries and your veins,
They could hang up and stop your blood
Like plugged up sewer drains.

"Then you'd need surgery
To get the blood on by.
Your life could be in danger.
You possibly could die."

I says, "Doc, I don't fear dying.
I've done most things I need to do.
I've checked this range pretty good,
Could move on to something new.

"It looks like this people pasture
Is darn near fully stocked.
I might look for greener pasture
If they leave the gate unlocked."

He says, "It ain't all that simple.
Dying ain't no joke.
You could only half die.
You could have a massive stroke.

"Then they'd take you to a nursing home,
Give you a chair with wheels.
Wash your face, and wipe your butt,
And feed you all your meals.

"Your kids would come to visit
And not know what to say.
And you'd look at a tile floor
Every day—all day.

"Your mouth will fall open, your tongue fall out,
They'll strap you in your chair.
Nice days your wife will push you round the block
So you can get fresh air."

I says, "Doc, I hear you.
It ain't a pretty scene.
I'll start walking on the treadmill,
That damnable machine.

"That sure would be no decent way
In which to treat a wife,
Who for over forty years
Has been the mainstay of your life.

"A wife who raised your kids
And washed your stinken' shorts.
And been a friend to your friends,
And done extras of all sorts.

"A wife that's made you happy
A wife that's made you proud,
A wife that checked the way you looked
When you went out in the crowd.

"Yes, Doc, I'll go walk on that belt
The belt that has no end.
Yes, Doc, two miles a day
I promise that I'll spend."

That belt, it is endless,
It's narrow and it's straight,
Like the path in the Bible
That leads to heaven's gate.

Is it the way to heaven?
I have no way to tell,
But I know I'll walk a treadmill
If I must go to hell.

STROKE

(7 months after Walk was written)

I thought I recognized the pain,
Though it was kind of soon,
For it was only nine o'clock
With hunger pangs like noon.

I fixed some toast and corn flakes
With a banana on the side,
And had a cup of, "Old Black Joe",
But the pain did not subside.

I headed for the office,
A little chore to do
And started feeling really sick,
Like I had a case of flu.

The room started spinning,
Like I had drank too much beer,
So I called Margaret to come
Clean the wax out of my ear.

I was feeling nauseated
And asked Margaret for a pan.
And I broke out in a sweat.
I could sure have used a fan.

I whoopsed up like a geyser,
But it didn't seem to help.
I was feeling pretty bad,
Sicker than a whelp.

I was seeing double
And the scene sure wasn't good.
Margaret was in her doctor book
Doing what a good wife should.

Christ & the Cowboy, 2nd Edition

We decided that my condition
Was beyond home remedy.
And that the hospital
Was where I'd ought to be.

They took a few blood samples,
Blood pressure, temp' and pulse.
Doc, said, "I think it is a stroke,"
Without waiting for results.

They put a needle in my arm,
And gave some kind of shot.
I was sweaty and clammy,
Like the weather was too hot.

They loaded me in the, "Red Wagon,"
But, they left the siren still,
And they pointed it for Billings.
The ride was all down hill.

Margaret picked up Rosina
And headed for Billings too.
On the way they called prayer chains.
That's how smart people do.

By the time I got to Billings,
My color was coming back.
I enjoyed the attention,
And tried some jokes to crack.

I guess I had a blood clot
That some how went away,
And in the log book of my life
It was my lucky day.

They did CAT, and MRI,
And every kind of test.
Of staff and equipment,
I feel I got the best.

Now, I'm in my room waiting
For when the doctor comes and talks
To see if I am going home,
Or should buy a padded box.

The personnel and equipment,
I am thankful they were there.
I'm thankful to all those who prayed.
And to the One who answers prayer.

August 31, 1998

PS   I just was ordered home.

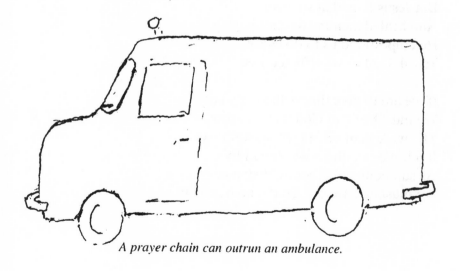

A prayer chain can outrun an ambulance.

HEALING

Grandpa God asked me to tell
How much He really wants us well.
Christ Jesus said to say,
"To wellness, He is the way."
The Spirit said that we should call
On Him for help if we should fall.

First in healing, we are taught
It's best if we brag on God a lot.
Tell Him what a great God He is
And how He really knows His biz.
And tell Him from the very start
How we love Him with all our heart.

When Adam ate the forbidden fruit
The seeds of sickness then took root.
But Jesus took that sin away
And healed men in His earthly stay.
He empowered us to do as He,
To ask God to set afflicted free.

If we are to give illness the Holy boot
We must bring to God its basic root.
The wrongs of others we must forgive
If a life of wellness we should live.
As surgeons scrub before they cut.
We must cleanse our hearts, no if, no but.

When we're in tune and the stage is set,
We must still ask for healing yet.
If we know the problem and where it's at,
We can ask the Spirit to tend to that.
If the cause and treatment we don't know,
We tell the problem, "In Jesus name it must go.

We must forgive ancestors of long ago
Of crippling bonds we do not know.
Jesus said the thing to do,
"Forgive as I have forgiven you."
For many an illness has been built
On anger, worry, stress, or guilt.

In healing the sick, it's also fair
To double team in this game of prayer.
Jesus said when believers can agree,
Even if only two or three,
I will do the things they claim,
If they but ask it in My Name.

If we see no healing of the flesh
We must go back and start afresh.
We might find something we have missed,
A festering thorn, a hidden cyst,
A bruise from some verbal stone,
Or fear of fighting life's fight alone.

With re–examination now complete,
Lay the problem back at Our Savior's feet.
We state again that we now claim
Healing and wellness in Jesus' name.
The words that Satan and demons fear
Is the name of Jesus in prayers they hear.

Christ & the Cowboy, 2nd Edition

So call on Jesus again and again.
And praise Him highly when we win.
Ask the Spirit to be in the doctor's eyes,
And in his hands, and to make him wise.
For the hands we use to touch the ill
Are the only hands to do God's will.

So pray for healing every day,
That pain and suffering be cast away.
Healing is for us to receive,
If the words of Jesus we believe.
Yes, Grandpa God wants us well
And all pain and sickness sent to hell.

JOKE

A friend of mine once told a joke
      About a preacher who one day,
Was calling on parishioners
      Who had seemed to drift away.

One man had a garden
      That made him stop and stare.
Its beauty and its bounty
      Showed the epitome of care.

The preacher said, "What a glorious garden
      You and the Lord have here.
The answer, "You should have seen it
      When God had it alone last year."

I laughed a kind of hollow laugh.
      This struck a tender cord.
I realized that I was guilty
      Of leaving it to the Lord.

He is faithful to His promises.
      He meets our every need.
But if we want good fruits and beauty
      WE must remove the weed.

That God will always do His share
      Is a fact I've always known,
And if I want the life abundant
      I must not leave Him alone.

WHERE IS THE CHURCH?

Some time ago
I was destined to go
To a church in a neighboring town.
By the stained glass and brick
I could recognize quick
That the proper address I had found.

The building I'd know
Held four hundred or so,
But only a dozen souls sat in the pews.
By some quirk of fate
Had I chose the wrong date
To come and hear The Good News?

I sat there alone
Asking what message is shown?
For what truth should I be in search?
For the building found here
Was worthy of cheer,
A fine building, but where is The Church?

For it is known
That mortar and stone
And stained glass impress our Lord not.
For since Adam and Eve
First our Father did grieve
It's been hearts of men He has sought.

I studied the wall
And tried to recall
How the bricks were laid one at a time,
How each brick touches six
Bound by a mortar mix
Of sand and cement and lime.

Then I started to see
How a strong church could be
Built just one soul at a time,
By one soul touching six
Bound by a mortar mix
Of love and sharing of time.

What the Father desires
Is people, not spires,
The hearts of those people He picks.
It's up to me and you
His mission to do
By each of us touching six.

TRINITY

A fellow I know once said to me,
"I don't dig this Holy Trinity.
What's all this Holy Spirit stuff?
Isn't praying to God the Father quite enough?
They say for gods we should have just one
So why The Spirit and The Son?"

Said I, "See that tractor over there?
It has one engine, is that fair?
Another thing that we both know–
It has four pistons that make it go.
If your prayers are just The Father and you
It's like that tractor hitting on just two.

You've got things going, that is true
But it's kind of kapuck, kapuck, kapoo.
Then as you learn about the game
You start to pray in Jesus' name.
That prayers are answered you will know
As in Jesus' name you onward grow."

And then you'll plug The Spirit in
And "Varoom" the wheels will start to spin,
And with the Triune Life of Grace
Miracles will soon be commonplace.
If we brag on God each time we pray
And stay out of The Father, Son, and Spirit's way
Then our prayer power can be put to use
And "The Will of God" can be turned loose.

The greatest problem with us all—
We try to keep our God too small.
The trouble with most of us and God—
We try to confine Him to a bod'.
Can you think of anything that's worse
For a God that can make a universe?

How can a God so large and mighty be
Able to get inside and clean an artery?
On a thing like this I wouldn't kid
For I know when He was asked and did.
No, we can't confine Him to a bod'
Not The Spirit part of God.

My friend said, "You lost me in the rush.
Didn't Jesus have a body of bones and flesh?"
Yes, He is the only one that history gave
Who took His body beyond the grave.
And if we heed the words He's spoken
We'd know that His body still is broken
For the redemption of our sin
Ever since He brought the custom in.

As the Sacrament goes into our gut
There is no if, no and, no but.
Jesus has entered the body of man,
So look for Him there whenever you can.
In your home or place of labor
Look for Jesus in your friend and neighbor.
With all this it's come to me
Thou shalt not explain The Trinity.

CHRISTMAS NAP

I had stretched out on the sofa
And settled in for a nap.
I dreamed I was a child again
Seated on Santa's lap.

He put his arm around me
And asked if I'd been good.
I said I'd fed the chickens
And fetched the coal and wood.

Then he asked what special gift
Would fill my heart with joy.
I said I was pretty well fixed for tack
And I didn't need a toy.

I looked Santa in the eye.
And said. "If you want the truth.
There's an old white horse down in the barn
With an ulcerated tooth.

I save the leaves from off the hay rack,
And steal some extra grain.
But to watch that old horse try to eat
You know he is in pain.

So Santa, if you are for real
And are serious at all,
Leave something for that old horse, Chief,
When he comes into his stall.

The old team, Dick and Diamond,
They've been awfully good to me,
And I'd be mighty happy
If they had something beneath the tree.

And our old dog, Rover,
A friend that's always there,
To not remember him
Would simply not be fair.

And the milk cow Judy,
She never moves away,
When I steal a bean can full of milk
In the middle of the day.

So give these animals a gift,
Please Santa if you would.
Because they are so special
And they are so good.

But, Santa, I'm a might confused,
And it makes me kind'a sad,
That God sent baby Jesus
Because people here were bad.

They say we all are sinners
No matter how hard we try,
But Jesus takes our sins away
And hides them in the sky.

Santa, I've a Mom and Dad,
A home with a stove and heat,
Warm clothes and wool blankets,
And lots of food to eat.

So, Santa, if in your magic bag,
You have a gift for me,
Just leave it beside some orphan's bed
Who doesn't have a tree.

And, Santa, if you see Lord Jesus,
As you travel on your way,
Would you give him something special,
Because it's HIS birthday."

OLD FRIEND

Old Friend, I can't remember
The first time that we met;
Yet, our being friends this long and all,
How could I forget?

So maybe now it's time to say
Some things not said before.
You've always been a true friend,
But an "Old Friend" means much more.

We've shared some special moments
In our lives, both good and bad.
We've rode life's trail together,
Shared any thing we had.

There was a lot of private talkin'
That never went past you and me,
Those talks with someone else, Old Friend,
Well, that just couldn't be.

Today, I could make a new friend
In a half a dozen ways,
But for a man to have an old friend
Takes a heap of yesterdays.

I can make a new friend tomorrow
Or most any future day,
But an old friend is tempered by fire and flood
And wrecks along the way.

So take care of yourself, Old Friend,
Please, for both our sakes,
Because another old friend like you,
I haven't got time to make.

SHEEP

He said to Pete, "Get off your duff.
Go feed those lambs the proper stuff.
I know that rooster means much to you
And woke you the second time he crew,
But now you have a job to keep.
Right now, Pete, go feed the sheep.

"Cows and bees give milk and honey,
And the fatted calf is worth much money.
But, Pete, the job for you today
Is to tend the flock lest one should stray.
No, Pete, there is no time for sleep,
The hour is now for tending sheep.

"Forsake hogs and goats at any cost
To see not a single lamb is lost.
The ass, as asses' fate shall be,
But all the sheep belong to me.
Rich the harvest I shall reap
If you, Pete, will tend my sheep."

Now, Pete gave a little laugh at best
And pointed a finger at his chest
And said, "Who me? You surely jest.
It's patching nets that I do best.
I fish waters wide and deep
Yet, you're asking me to go feed sheep?"

And the Man said, "Simon, son of John,
It's up to you when I am gone
To be my shepherd round the clock,
To feed and multiply my flock.
You say your love for me is deep.
If you really love me, feed my sheep."

The thing that wakes me from my sleep—
Am I a Peter or a sheep?
Or, am I better classed indeed
With the turkeys that scratch for feed?
If I, Lord, can your commandments keep,
Would you choose me, Lord, to be a sheep?

Am I a wolf with bloody chin
For not repenting my way of sin?
Am I a serpent, despised by all,
Because I caused someone to fall?
Lord, please come and shepherd me
That I, among your lambs may be.

Am I like an eagle who high can soar
But dare not pass through the narrow door?
Am I like a rodent that hides by day,
Can't stand your light to lead my way?
Lord, lead me where the pasture's green,
Beside still waters, cool, and clean.

If I'm a lamb, then give to me
A lamb's meekness and humility.
If, Lord, a shepherd I should be,
Oh, what a great responsibility
On this lowly servant you would heap
Of asking me to tend Your sheep.

That not a lamb be lost or fall
For You are shepherd of us all.
That all of us may without shame
Answer when you call our name.
When you count your sheep, Lord, by and by,
 Then may I answer, "Here am I."

ROWBOAT OF LIFE

Life is like a rowboat.
The oars are in my hand.
I have to cross the sea of life
To reach the promised land.

I can't see where I'm going—
Only from whence I came.
To not go in a circle
I must pull each oar the same.

One oar is work and drudgery;
The other is play and fun.
A never–ending circle
Is a life of only one.

At times I've put more effort
To pulling on one oar,
Then found that I have turned off course
Toward a barren rocky shore.

I must turn and look behind me
To see what lies ahead,
For what I see as I pull those oars
Is what is past and dead.

But if I lose sight of what I know
With faith, as fact and true,
How can I keep direction
In the sea I'm passing through?

Now, suppose I saw a stranger
Clinging to a tree,
Would I change my course to pick him up
And say, "Get in with me?"

Then, as he'd get into my boat,
We'd be seated face to face,
And he could guide me as I'd row,
To reach that promised place.

He might say, "Rough waters lie ahead.
Hold a little to your right.
It's best to take them head on,
So pull with all your might."

And when I'd used up all my strength,
He'd say, "Now sea be still."
Dare I say, "Who is this man,
That the sea obeys His will?"

And suppose He said, "Stop rowing now.
We'll walk from here on in."
Have I the faith to leave the boat
And put that much trust in Him?

I might say, "Lord, this sort of thing
I know you've done before,
But there is sure a lot of water
Between this boat and shore.

"This boat is like my body.
I'd hate to leave it now.
I know I will not need it there,
But, I feel safer here somehow.

"So, please, Lord, be patient.
Wait for me at the shore.
'Cause, Lord, I'd like a few more years
Of pulling on these oars."

TEEPEE

Once upon a time, there were two young trees. Actually, there was a whole forest of trees, but these two trees were attracted to each other. They waved to each other every morning, and whispered to each other in the evening breeze. They very much wanted to be together, but they had roots and couldn't even touch branches. One day they could stand it no longer and gave up their roots and branches and became poles. They bound themselves together, but they could only support each other in one direction, and they were very unsteady. They felt that they had made a terrible mistake.

One day, they saw another pole about their size. They invited it to join with them so they would support each other and not fall. They bound themselves together near the top and spread apart at the bottom. They were very strong, each leaning on the other two, each supporting the other two. The third pole was God and the bond that tied them together was marriage. They were so strong that other poles could be laid against them and they began to take the shape of a teepee. The other poles did not have to be bound, just laid in place. These poles were extended family, friends, jobs, neighbors, a home and mortgage, all the extras that make the marriage package complete. Finally, with all the poles properly spaced around the first three, it was covered with the blanket of life.

There was an entrance at the bottom and a small vent opening at the top for the foul air to escape through. The bottom opening had a flap that could be closed for protection, privacy, and warmth.

In the center of the marriage teepee is the fire of intimacy, of love, of shared dreams, and close moments. It is a fire that needs to be tended often. Some times it only needs to be stirred; some times it needs more fuel.

The poles protrude beyond the bonding point. This portion of the pole supports nothing; contributes nothing, other than being there should the knot slip. This is also symbolic of the personal freedom and independence that every party of a marriage must have.

And so marriage is like a teepee, a man, a woman, and God each depending on the others and on the bond of marriage. On this simple tripod hangs our very civilization.

THE FIRST HOMEMAKER
OR
MRS. GOD CREATED WOMAN IN HER OWN IMAGE

In the beginning God created the earth,
I'm sure you've heard this stuff.
And then God said that it was good.
Mrs. God said, "Not good enough."

She looked at this thing that God had made
And said, somewhat annoyed,
"But, what good is it?
It is without form and void."

So, God put back on His apron,
And took earth in His hand,
And God made a firmament,
And oceans and dry land.

But Mrs. God wasn't satisfied
And said, "Oh, what a shame,
For, every time I see this earth,
It always looks the same."

So, God started earth to spinning
And that caused nights and days,
Then He had it loop around the sun,
And tilt in different ways.

This sort of pleased Mrs. God.
She saw mountains capped with snow,
And the other side of earth
Flowers and grass would grow.

She saw jungles in the middle,
And icebergs at the poles.
Then God made Her some volcanoes
That erupted fiery coals.

She'd ask God to move a mountain,
Or perhaps dry up a sea,
Or maybe make a desert
Where a forest used to be.

Then God filled the earth with critters
Of different size and shapes
From guppies up to elephants,
And pelicans to apes.

Then God said, "I'll take another day,
And spend it making man.
I'll make him better than these critters,
As like Me as I can,"

Well, God worked real hard on man
And gave the job His best.
By evening God was tuckered
And He had to stop and rest.

Now, Mrs. God saw Him working,
And She studied all His charts.
She said, "I can do better
If I change some moving parts.

"I'll leave off all the face hair...
Use a little bit smaller mold...
Make smoother curves and softer...
More comfortable to hold.

"God made man much too violent,
The way he fights, and hunts, and kills.
I'll make woman more submissive...
Wanting niceties and frills."

But, Mrs. God was temperamental,
And had Her times of stress,
Some times She had hot flashes,
Or was it P.M.S.?

Christ & the Cowboy, 2nd Edition

Once She turned off all the heaters,
And opened up all the doors
That caused a Great Ice Age,
And froze God's dinosaurs.

God always had His honey–do's,
Just like modern married man.
She'd say, "Will You fix this for Me?
You're so mighty, I know You can."

But, some times She'd view God's efforts
With resentment and disgust
"I asked Him to lower Mount Saint Helens;
Now look at all this dust.

"And His automatic sprinkler...
The one that controls the rains...
It makes floods in Louisiana,
And leaves dry spots in the plains."

She created woman in Her image,
And then, by coincidence,
She taught woman how to pray
And God hasn't rested since.

I'M YOUR HOME

Dear special family,

Thank you for buying me.
Thank you for loving me.
I'm your home.

Thank you for maintaining me
Thank you for blessing me
I'm your home.

I promise that I will keep you warm.
I'll be your refuge in the storm.
I'm your home.

I'll be your quiet place to rest.
I'll open my arms out to your guest.
I'm your home.

I'll protect you when you sleep.
And all your private secrets keep.
I'm your home.

I'll be where God can talk to you
And Christ and the Holy Spirit too.
I'm your home.

Thank you for having me Blessed
To be worthy, I'll do my best.
I love being your home.

For a special house blessing.

BABYLON AND PENTECOST

A bunch of us were talking
About the days of old.
About Babylon and Pentecost
And stories we were told.

About how at Babylon
Men no longer could converse,
And how then at Pentecost
The process was reversed.

How men from different places,
Who were professors of the Word,
Could speak in their native dialect
And in a common tongue be heard.

Were the gifts of the Holy Spirit
At the time of Pentecost
To be with believers forever
Or with that generation lost?

I believe that the Holy Spirit
And His gifts abide today,
And the common tongue of
Pentecost in a very subtle way.

For you see each member of our group
Had come from a different place—
As Anglican, Roman, and Methodist,
Yet we share a common grace.

We say different words in liturgy
Yet they all come out the same.
Be we Catholics or Protestants
We praise God in Jesus' name.

Were the gifts of the Holy Spirit
For one generation to receive?
No, they are for all of us
Who in the Giver do believe.

But there is one condition;
There is one string attached.
We could have it all, but without "Love"
The whole shebang is scratched.

HAWK CREEK FIRE

Margaret Murphy's thoughts during and after the fire, put to poetry by Chuck.

The Bulls were tinder dry;
The threat of fire was real.
Word that one was on a neighbor
Meant a need with which to deal.

The fire was not on our land,
But it wasn't very far.
Chuck took tools and the pickup;
I put food into the car.

There were cats and the county grader
And farm tractors on the line.
There were trucks with pumps and water
And men with shovels came behind.

The wind was causing trouble.
The lines were hard to keep.
But they'd have it held by morning
Though we all would lose some sleep.

We got word of new breakouts.
The wind was getting mean.
It torched over on the west end
And was now on John's fourteen.

Chuck had gone down on the east front
To help those neighbors with their fight
By walking before the dozer
To guide it in the night.

Fire was on the South, the East and West.
I now was home alone.
That Roens lost their home and buildings
at this time now was known.

A young man was badly burned.
He probably would die.
"Dear God, protect the others,"
I had a little cry.

It was crowning out and jumping
Is what we wives were told.
Then again the word came in
The fire line didn't hold

Where this fire would stop
No one seemed to know.
By now two–thirds of the sky
Had a reddish orange glow.

It was now in Carter's Coolie
Where the fuel was prime.
It could go to the river
If it chose to in its time.

"Dear Lord, I'll give the West End
If this fire it must claim,
But please, Lord, spare my home,
I ask in Jesus name."

I decided what important things
For survival I must do.
For help I called our daughter
It was night time, about two

We loaded up the treasures,
Things we could not replace
Into two empty trailers
That still were on the place.

Hours had blended into days:
Account of time was lost.
Just do the thing that needed done
And disregard the cost.

Christ & the Cowboy, 2nd Edition

Help showed up out of nowhere,
My sister and my brother,
A friend along with his friend,
Another friend and still another.

The fire came across the ridge.
The flames leaped high in view
I said, "There is the fire.
Dear God, Where are you?"

Rosina was on the telephone
One message quick to say,
"My Mom's home is in danger:
Call the prayer chain and pray."

Then in a few long minutes
There was a change of wind.
The fire turned back along itself
To where it had already been.

I thanked God for this short reprieve.
I turned around and then,
I saw God in the faces
Of two score of determined men.

I heard the voice of the Almighty
In the graders and the cats.
And felt the Spirit of living water
In trucks ready to go to bat.

I saw God in my sister
Cleaning carrots at the sink.
Prepare food for the fighters
Was all that she could think.

I saw Christ in the couple
Who came all the way from Beach (ND).
Carried water in a bucket
Where their hose just wouldn't reach.

The fire line finally held,
didn't blacken my precious view.
In each of the precious people
I know, Dear God are You.

I heard the voice of Jesus
From the mouth of those who'd care
And phone to sincerely offer
In some way our cross to bear.

Then the gifts of charity
Started coming in
I knew, God, That in the hearts of men
Is where you've always been.

"Thanks, Lord, for the lesson.
To remember it I'll try.
I know now where you are Lord.
Please know, Lord, here am I".

CHRISTMAS 97

Laid back in my chair
Thinking about what I want to do.
I want to write a Christmas poem,
But, with thoughts anew.

There are thousands of ways
The story is told,
The story that is now
Two thousand years old.

How the Inn was full,
No room for a stranger;
How a star led wise men
To the Baby in a manger.

They brought the Child gifts,
Which started the trend,
Of buying special gifts
To give or to send.

I sit here thinking, pondering,
And wondering why
We don't think and give more,
Of gifts we don't have to buy.

So get a pencil and pad,
And try to keep track,
Of the smiles that you give,
And those you get back.

Be sure to keep score,
Mark down on your list,
If you returned equal value
Every time you were kissed.

A hug is a gift
That has no price,
But is returned back in kind,
Compounded twice.

And so when Christians
All over the earth
Exchange gifts to honor
Our Dear Savior's birth,

Give generously the gift
That He told us to,
"Love one–another
As I have loved you."

© Rosiha

CHRISTMAS 98

I'm sitting in my easy chair
In the comfort of our home
Trying to think of how to start
This year's Christmas poem.

Some folks seem to think
The Christmas story should begin
In a little Mid East village
With three camel riding men.

How they brought gifts to a Baby
Of myrrh, gold, and frankincense,
Or the light they saw from heaven,
Not seen before nor since.

Others think that the story
Really should begin
With a couple sent to the stable
From an over crowded inn.

Or how the loving mother
Looked upon her Child so sweet
As she examined every feature
And His little hands and feet.

And that the story should go on
About this gifted Kid,
How He taught in the temple
And the wondrous things He did.

How He was named the Jewish King
Though He never wore a sword,
For He won all His conflicts
By the wisdom of His word.

How He was loved by many
Though He never took a wife.
How He walked earth for thirty years,
Less than half a normal life.

How He was to die upon the cross
And arise on Easter Day,
So the sins of those who confess His name
Will be forgiven... washed away.

If that's the story of Jesus
How His life did begin,
How, then, do I end this poem?
How does the Jesus story end?

IT DOESN'T

BRINGING IN THE DRILL

You button up your collar
Against the evening chill,
But you feel warm inside you
'Cause you're bringing in the drill.

You see a storm cloud building
Like the sides are going to spill,
And a rain would be most welcome
'Cause you're bringing in the drill.

You chose the best land on the farm,
The best to plow and till,
And did your best to work it right,
Used all your farming skill.

You borrowed money for fuel and parts
And the fertilizer bill,
And bought the best seed you could get
And put it through the drill.

It's up to God to sprout those seeds,
And you have faith He will,
And when it's time you'll spray for weeds,
And hope to get a kill.

You can curse and swear or kneel in prayer,
Be that what it will,
The crop is sown and God alone
Can make it stool and fill.

You can pray that hoppers don't prevail
And that moisture comes as rain not hail,
For good prices at the mill,
But the way it stands it's in God's hands
After bringing in the drill.

The governor opens a little bit
As you're starting up the hill,
The tractor, too, seems happy
That you're bringing in the drill.

You give the throttle an extra notch
She's barking loud and shrill
And trying hard to tell the world
That you're bringing in the drill.

The wife and kids are waving,
And your eyes begin to fill,
As you realize how you love them
As you're bringing in the drill.

The kids have done the milking,
But old Bossy lingers still
To share in the excitement
Of bringing in the drill.

You turn off the ignition.
Now all is quiet and still.
You're dirty, hungry, tired
From a long day with the drill.

You know that supper's waiting,
And you're going to eat your fill
'Cause you're at peace with God and man
After bringing in the drill.

APPENDIX

When I recite to groups, they seem to enjoy the poem more if I explain how it was inspired or motivated. I will try to write a short account of how each or at least most of my writing came about.

Rancher's Prayer Of Thanksgiving, page 10: In 1964, I was president of The Musselshell Valley Stockgrowers. As most organizations we changed presidents but the secretary had been there it seemed like for ever. We were planning the upcoming fall banquet and she asked who I wanted to ask to give the blessing. I said, What?" She asked again what minister I wanted to give a blessing. I said that I felt that the membership were all God loving, God fearing people and I didn't like having to bring in a "Hired Gun" to pray for us. She said, "OK you're it." I figured I should write something down so that I wouldn't get a brain cramp. About four lines, and I realized that I was writing a poem. This is what I gave that night, and it is my favorite prayer yet.

When God Made Montana, page 12: A challenge poem: I attended a self–improvement seminar at Montana State College, Bozeman, and we were to introduce ourselves, state our occupation and avocation or hobby. I said that I was a rancher and that I wrote poetry. I was challenged to write a fresh poem for closing.

Calistia Jane Cooley's Prayer, page 14: I have no idea when my Great Grandmother wrote this. I did know her, but didn't know about the poem until long after she was gone.

God Never Made, page 15: I was thinking about a little Ponderosa Pine tree that was growing out of a crack in a huge rock shelf. It was less than two feet tall and the stem was no larger than my finger, yet it was probably 30 to 50 years old. It had been about the same for the over 20 years that I had ridden that pasture. It was isolated from the larger healthier 60 to 70 year old trees, probably sprouted from the same seed drop, separated by bare sand and stone. A fire had killed the surrounding trees yet this little miracle survived.

Boots, page 16: I use this poem as an example of "Poetic License" when I do a program with grade school students. It is a true story except that both boots were brown and I didn't realize it until a friend came up after the service and said, "I bet you have another pair like that at home." We laughed, and he asked if the new boot didn't feel different than the old one. It did, but I thought that it was because a cow had stepped on my foot the day before and it was swollen.

Computers In Heaven, page 18: I had upgraded my computer, but not my skills. This poem resulted from trying to get Chuck and Windows 95 in synch.

Birth And Death, page 19: The 17 year old boy of a family of six was taken suddenly. The family was strong Christian. The grieving was great. God used me to tell the siblings to remember their mother placing their little hands on her stomach to feel the movement of the little child inside. This helped them accept that their brother was all right. Many years later I wrote the poem.

Range Boss, page 20. Another true poem granted poetic license. The horse was named Sunshine. The experience of the cowboy known as Me was real, portrayed in imagery.

John–Fifteen–One, page 24: I think that it was Jesus who said, "Welcome Back." It may have been an angel sent by him. I hope to ask Him some day. I have a friend who has orange groves. He points out that "sweet" fruit won't survive on it's own root and must be grafted to "sour–root" stock to produce "good fruit." During the time it is cut off, it is dead and dependent on someone to bring it back to the vine.

Life Without Jesus, page 27: In early assembling the material for this second addition, I found a blank page at this spot.

When Were You Saved, page 28: Some denominations feel that there must be a chronological moment in one's life when he or she was saved. To me that moment is better described as when they knew that they had accepted salvation.

Faith & Fact, page 30: Is the way it was, and speaks for its self.

Summer Ride, page 32: Some young adults were arguing, or conversing on what they called, "True Baptism." They didn't ask my opinion, but I wrote it down for my own satisfaction.

Cowboy's View On Abortion, page 39: As we were getting the first edition of *Christ and the Cowboy* ready for print, I woke up with this poem in my mind. I wrote it, took it to the printer, and we both felt God wanted it in the book.

Once Upon A Time, page 40: A Christmas poem.

Faithful One, page 42: We were having a Group Reunion after a spiritual weekend. This one fellow who had been a wife–beater bragged about how he didn't beat his wife any more and how he took his dog out in the country so it could run and be free of it's kennel. However, he refused to baby–sit their child or allow his wife to hire a baby–sitter so she could attend her Group

Reunion.

How I Pray, page 44: I met a person whom I knew in the hall of a convention center. "Chuck, do you know how to pray? Will you pray for my nephew? He has just been shot in the head." We prayed in the hall. The boy was back in school the next week. That incident motivated this poem.

Blind, page 46: A true short story. I tried many times to put this story into poem form, but nothing came out right. We are all blind to some degree.

Money, page 50: Money is god to some but not to Grandpa God.

First Thessalonians 5–26 KJV, page 51: What happens when a cowboy reads the Bible.

Platelets, page 52: Started out to be a satire on the personal questions asked when we donate blood or blood products.

Roses Are Red, page 55: When things get quiet my youngest grand son asks me to tell a poem. We were in church Easter Sunday and things were quiet. I made up the first verse of this and then the service started.

Landmark, page 56, and *Somebody's Grandmother's Chair*, page 58, are included not because they are so spiritual, as because they reflect different attitudes toward things of the past generations.

Somebody's Grandmother's Chair, page 58: see above.

Meaning Of Christmas, page 60: Another Christmas poem.

Grandpa God, page 62: Just as it states after, *"Money."*

Cone Tree, page 64: Inspired by the event, and the thought of how many trees die in our Christmas celebrations.

Young Woman, page 66: Inspired by a witness talk.

My Walk In Faith, page 68: My answer to myself of why I believe.

Caught, page 73: Inspired by the statement, "It wasn't what he did, it was that he got caught."

Who And What, page 73: A true incident that I felt was worth recording in a poem.

Women Of The Church, page 74: Inspired after two opposing female factions asked my opinion of how a guild room should be redone. Hug 'em and run.

Auction Barn, page 76: I love the imagery of this poem and it relates the fact that a cowboy won't roast his boss unless he likes and respects him.

Walk, page 81: Not particularly spiritual, but sets the stage for the next poem.

Stroke, page 85: Shows the strength of a prayer chain.

Healing, page 88: The most recent poem in this book: I was at a weekend seminar for lay healing ministry. We concluded with Communion on Sunday. Some years ago, I read where we should bring a gift to Grandpa God much as we would bring a gift if we were going to Grandma's house for Sunday dinner. I have given all of my family members, reserving only the right to continue to love them. I have given problems and problem people, blessings and treasures. Twenty years of communions, and I have given a lot of people and things away so some times I have to ask God what He wants. This day, I heard one of the few audible answers to prayer. I heard, *"Poem."* I said, "What?" I heard, *"Poem,"* again and saw a scrap of paper going past the altar.

Joke, page 91: Speaks for itself.

Where Is The Church, page 92: A true incident.

Trinity, page 94: Another way to explain the Trinity.

Christmas Nap, page 96: Another Christmas poem.

Old Friend, page 99: Several of us were discussing the loss of a friend. One man expressed his grief in the form of anger. He felt betrayed. He said: "I can't live long enough to make a friend like him."

Sheep, page 100: Meditation on a lonely night when the family was living in town for school.

Rowboat Of Life, page 102: When the family was in town for school, I was lonely and depressed. Financially we were in a tight situation, and it seemed that every thing I tried slid us back farther. I thought if I just turned around, then sliding backward would get me where I wanted to be. A rowboat is the only thing that I know of that gets where you want to go by going back-wards. I started to write a satire. When I picked the stranger off the tree, I thought he might be some kind of Ag. consultant. I didn't think about it being Jesus until He calmed the water.

Teepee, page 104: A thought that wouldn't come out as a poem.1

The First Homemaker, page 106: An occasional poem is

one written for an occasion. We had a friend who was the president of the five–county regional Homemakers' Clubs. She asked me to provide some noon entertainment for their regional meeting in our county, and perhaps I could write something new just for them. This was for that occasion.

I Am Your Home, page 109: Written for a house blessing.

Babylon And Pentecost, page 110: About how small the differences between denominations really are, and the Gifts of the Spirit today.

Hawk Creek Fire, page 112: My wife's thoughts during the fire that took one life, 29 homes and over 170,000 acres of forest and grass. The adversity of nature brings out the best in people.

Christmas 97, page 116: Another Christmas poem.

Christmas 98, page 118: Another Christmas poem.

Bringing In The Drill, page 120: Closure of the job at hand, and being at peace knowing that you did the best you could.

Made in United States
Troutdale, OR
11/09/2023

14422721R00083